❧ *The Land of Bliss*

Pitt Poetry Series
Ed Ochester, Editor

The Land of Bliss

Cathy Song

University of Pittsburgh Press

The publication of this book is supported by a grant from the Pennsylvania Council of the Arts.

Published by the University of Pittsburgh Press,

Pittsburgh, Pa. 15260

Copyright © 2001, Cathy Song

All rights reserved

Manufactured in the United States of America

Printed on acid-free paper

10 9 8 7 6 5 4 3 2 1

ISBN 0-8229-5770-1

To Ulu Garmon, Priscilla Hoback,
Wayne Morioka, and Noriko Saimo
    guardians at the gate

To Douglas
    who has the touch

To Juliet
    sono-mama

    in love and gratitude

For Samuel McHarg

Contents

꩜ *Fetters*

Pokanini Girl   3

The Pineapple Fields   5

The Girl Can Run   7

Stink Eye   11

Pa-ke   14

Ghost   16

My Mother's Name   19

Living Proof   21

The Child Floats in a Sea of Grass   26

What Is Given   28

Fetters   29

꩜ *The Roses of Guadalajara*

She Meant to See China   33

The Valley Boat   36

Stone Soup   38

Committed   39

The Expense of Mildew   40

Fragrance Is the First to Go   42

Rust   43

Horizon   45

Riverbed   46

Peacefully, on the Wings of Forgiveness   47

Blue   49

The Roses of Guadalajara   50

✻ *White Ashes*

Mountains of Ash 55

A Poet in the House 62

Book of Hours 63

Blueroses 64

The Sister 67

Honored Guest 73

In the Far Wing of an Old Museum 75

A City of Sleeves 77

The Slow Upheaval of Mist 82

The Sky-Blue Dress 83

Fur 86

White Ashes 88

✻ *The Land of Bliss*

The Last of My Chinese Uncles
   Enters the Gates of Heaven 93

Triptych 96

The Bodhisattva Muses 100

Mother of Us All 104

Out of the Broken Mirror 106

Angels on the Way to the Dalai Lama 110

Handful 112

Caldera Illumina 113

The Land of Bliss 121

Acknowledgments 123

Fetters

Once I was blessed;
I was awaited like the rain.
　　　—Joni Mitchell

Pokanini Girl

Pokanini girl,
she so skinny!
Pokanini girl,
wear size two bikini.

When she lie down,
she flat like one penny.
No can tell da front from da back.
Where stay her okole?

Pokanini girl,
she so frail!
No can do nutting,
no can even pound one nail.

She so white!
Her skin so pale!
When she take one bath,
her tan wash off jes l'dat!

Hard fo hit
when we play dodgeball.
Pokanini girl,
her shadow so small!

Always in da corner,
stay daydream.
She one loser.
We no like her on our team.

She so weak!
No can shout.
Ho da pipsqueak!
Her mouth try open but nutting come out.

Her madda stay worry.
Her fadda stay broke.
No mo vitality,
everyting stay choke.

Pokanini girl!
Come on, no be l'dat.
No be scared, Pokanini girl.
Nobody going hurt you.

The Pineapple Fields

Father rescued us from the pineapple fields.
We were certain to be lost in the pineapple fields.
We were wayward, barefoot, and undisciplined in the pineapple fields.
Hunters of mongoose, we wore rags, were red dirt streaked
like savages in the pineapple fields.
He saved us from living and dying in the pineapple fields.
The pineapple fields were a place to flee from,
a place plagued with black feathers,
blood of the rooster spray painted like graffiti
across chicken coop houses fenced by a junkyard of cars,
cannibalized for parts.
Scrawny kids with uku lived in the pineapple fields,
kids who by age six had as many gold
teeth as pool hall uncles down on Hotel Street,
teeth gone bad by way of termites
like their untended houses,
all of them
rotten to the core.
The day we left the pineapple fields
Mother cried.
Violet, Martha, and Lorraine stood in the driveway
of our mildew-infested house to wave good-bye.
They gathered communal tears
that stung like wedding rice.
They bid us farewell.
We left the pineapple fields for the city,
a haole neighborhood of swimming pools
and Filipino gardeners silently trimming
a legacy of Saturday morning lawns.
No wonder Mother cried.
How would she ever keep up?
No more morning coffee brewing for talks at Violet's,
no more humming of Lorraine's sewing machine
whipping up creamy ball gowns for our dolls,

no more Mr. Suzuki's shakuhachi sighing through the mock
   orange hedge.
Don't act like you just came from the pineapple fields
meant we couldn't wear anything purple,
couldn't loop strings of Christmas lights
like fishnets around picture windows all year long,
couldn't get too dark in the summer,
couldn't yell "Mommy! Telephone!" at the top of our lungs,
couldn't slap our thighs and howl with unbecoming laughter,
couldn't beg Mommy for candy at the pharmacy,
couldn't pour shoyu on our rice, ketchup on our eggs,
couldn't think Flamingo's Chuck Wagon the greatest place to
   eat anymore.
Don't talk like you came from the pineapple fields
meant we couldn't talk with our mouths
full of broken sentences,
couldn't shove "yuh?" like food
heaped onto spoons.
Don't talk like you just came from the pineapple fields
meant we had to speak proper English.
We remained silent instead,
our tongues harnessed by the foreign shoelaces of syntax
restrictive as the new shoes Father brought home for us to wear.

The Girl Can Run

The girl can run.
We marvel
at her tongue.
As fast as her little
legs can carry her
she runs.
She is running
as fast as
her little legs
can carry her
up over the hill
and out of the town.
The girl
can run.
We marvel
at her
tongue,
lizard-quick,
bufo in the bathhouse
lapping up the flies.
Same little girl who shouted
see me see that star?
She's damned if
she doesn't
make it that far.
She's hoarded words,
stuffed and stitched
her own tough hide.
Old man on the porch swing
doesn't give a shit.
Save it
for yourself,
the old man spits.
The girl can
run. We marvel at her

tongue.
Little legs,
plump and flea-bitten,
pump on the sputter
of heart's broken wheel.
Puff puff she pants.
See me see me dance
over the hill
out of the town
past Mother
screaming fists into sheets.
There!
on the clothesline—
so shame!—
everybody can see
all the brown stains.
Puff puff she pants.
See me see me dance
past Sister's kookoo marbles
rolling shut behind
a doll's dull lid.
Nothing to see inside
her head.
Old man spits,
save yourself.
I've got my own
noise to take to bed.
The girl can run.
We marvel at her tongue.
She takes the short
cut, the cleverest route.
Mean is the speed of her tongue.
Puff puff she pants,
sucking up the air.
All the air
she sucks into her lungs
and runs.

Move out of her way.
Here she comes.
Bufo in the bathhouse
bloats immense on flies.
Tongue turning stones to bread crumbs.
Badly, has she said it?—
she wants to come home.
At the heart is the fiction
it's only flies.
Shoo! Shoo! Shoo!
At the heart is the drama
of the unloved child.
Now it's spoken—
has she said it?—badly,
she wants to come home.
Here she comes,
pursued by invisible matter.
Flies in the bathhouse
quiver under lies.
No telling
what's behind her.
Invisible matter
carries its own
noise inside
her head.
A sputtering of fists and crazy laughter.
Are you listening, Mother?
Invisible matter
gobbling her up.
She'll run us over,
peel the skin of the darkest
berries to steal
the darkest stories.
She's damned if she doesn't
take it
that far.
See me see that star.

Gobble us up into crumbs and chatter.
Late nights,
after dinner,
feasted and content,
what-flies-off-the-toothpick-
loose-and-careless
chatter.
The girl can run.
We are struck by the marvel of her tongue.

Stink Eye

Somebody been giving you Stink Eye?
Let me tell you about Stink Eye.
Stink Eye no mean nothing
when you owe somebody money.
Pay up, girl. No be in debt.
But Stink Eye means something
when you owe somebody nothing.
Remember when Connie Mamazuka, the girl with the mustache,
grabbed your lipstick in the PE locker room
and smeared it all over her big fat lips?
Wasn't 'cause she like your lipstick.
Was 'cause you was one cute skinny chick.
She was giving you Stink Eye all along
and you never even know it.
Now you know it
and now you watch for it.
You was always catching Stink Eye,
always crying to your mother about somebody
icing you out.
When Stink Eye is cold, it is fucking freezing,
it can make you shiver and cry,
"But Mommy, Mommy, what did I do?"
Took you long time to know
you never do nothing
but you was good at something,
something Stink Eye like try steal
not 'cause Stink Eye going use it.
Stink Eye just no like
you use it
'cause if you use it
only going make Stink Eye feel
more ugly, feel more stupid.
Easy for spot
Stink Eye coming from one mousy thing.
More tricky for spot

Stink Eye coming from some of the friendliest faces.
And you the dumb one, left dazed and hurt.
"But she seemed so sympathetic."
Yeah, right.
Stink Eye sideswipes into you
out of nowhere
where somebody been thinking
evil thoughts about you,
wishing bad luck to blow bad breath upon you,
knock you down,
forget your words,
drop your tools,
make you sputter and drool.
Under the bed,
in Stink Eye's room,
get one picture of you
stabbed like one pin cushion
with so many needles, stabbed
like one cactus, stabbed like one porcupine.
Stink Eye even dreams about you.
Careful of that coat you wear,
the one you blossom in, feel loved in,
the one that keeps you warm.
Stink Eye like snatch it right off you
'cause Stink Eye just no can stand to see
you look so cool.
Stink Eye wants a piece of you.
So choose to be naive, girl, or wake up
'cause Stink Eye been waiting to sit on your chest,
pounce on your flesh,
squeeze the living air right out of you,
watch you flatten like one used-up tube of toothpaste.
Suck up your goodies,
Glutton-of-Stink-Eye,
ready to gorge on your talents,
feast on your fears.
So girl, run fast, spell good, write well, add up, think quick,

talk sharp, walk pretty, jump high, throw hard, sing sweet,
leap far.
Now you know it
and now you watch for it
'cause Stink Eye gets bigger and meaner and stronger
as you get better and smarter and stronger.
Scary thing about Stink Eye,
Stink Eye always looking for more—
as much as you willing to give.

Pa-ke

Pa-ke smells like my Uncle Sonny Boy's
breath ten years after his death
I can walk up the stairs of his
second-floor apartment
overlooking River Street
where old men play checkers
and spit caramel coins of sputum,
sticky as gau
his widow Auntie Siu Ching
still serves up every year of
the dog or dragon or monkey—
the pyramid of tangerines spirals
like ancient temples on her table,
banners of incense lean in the ashes
of a peach can beside the oily
pagodas of gin tui,
doughnuts that leave
my hands as greasy as her hair
after frying the graveyard shift
of hamburgers for minimum wage.
It beats going blind
over the thousand stitches
it used to take her to make a shorty mu'u.
Pa-ke, I never wanted to be.
Uncooperative,
I climbed the stairs behind Mother,
who made sure I too wore red,
her lips flaming like an azalea
as she greeted her aunt and uncle,
my great ancestors,
their greeting louder than fireworks
that chased all but the stout away.
So Pa-ke made me queasy
as the jai I stuffed into my mouth,

the vegetarian strands of monk's food
I mistook for the priest's hair,
pulling the fungus threads
through my teeth like floss
when Mother wasn't looking.
Pa-ke, not me,
you must be mistaken,
if Pa-ke meant Uncle Sonny Boy's
apartment, jammed with canned goods
like a warehouse in Kaka'ako
as if in preparation for another communist invasion.
On the walls a decade
of Narcissus Queens smiled from calendars,
modern beatific Kuan Yins
in Peking Opera fuchsia cheongsams.
Not even their stylized beauty,
perfect as the fragrant paper-whites
promising prosperity,
could make me Pa-ke.

Ghost

1.
Yellow ghost,
I flutter like a moth
invisible to these
children of soldiers,
dusting camphor wings,
pollen from the ancient pages

of poems, texts
that have no meaning
to the alley maps
of fast food and hard

cash, trash on the heels
of their need to go fast—

so very fast,
I am a blur to them,

without scent, a ghost
they rush right through

the light
I am so confident
I shed.

Who called the ghost white?

Yellow face of the oppressor—
one of a long line of Asian
schoolteachers who have stood before them,
yardstick in hand to measure
how far
they fail to measure up.

I say I am different.
I offer them
a jeweled seeded fruit,
a poem I pare and peel
that has no flesh.
It tastes like nothing
they want to eat.

2.
Bok gwai,
my mother called
the round eye,
persons of a certain
body odor—
a pungent offense
to the delicate flower of her nostrils.

Bok gwai filled flesh
more than any ghost
I could conjure,
noisy and hairy,
they moved visibly
with authority
in the world they were
so sure
belonged to them.

Bok gwai, white ghost,
she chose to call them.
By choosing, she chose
not to see
them
as she so surely saw
she was not seen.

Eyes sunken into
the bone hood of their skulls,
how could they possibly see?

But I saw,
and I liked
what I saw,
the round-eyed men
with golden fur on their arms.
They moved like soldiers
who on leave toss a confetti
of coins and candy
and cigarettes
to the waving sea of the weak,
the conquered, the invisible.

When I caught and brought
a round eye home,
my mother recoiled
at the sharp
scent of his skin.
It was the odor
of a meat eater,
unwashed flesh
she shrank from.
He had an earnest appetite
and good horse teeth.
His bite was strong.
He got under her yellow skin.
She invited him back again.
She said she liked the way
he chewed his bone.

My Mother's Name

Let's hear it
from Linda and Lori,
Debbie and Suzie,
pals I tossed
the five-pointed stars of jacks
with and won spare change
Around the World
with my fist,
clattering down broken sidewalks
on metal skates, the key
to my escape dangling like a cross
on a dog tag chain,
the fences that linked our houses and names.
What was my mother dreaming
as she ironed my father's shirts?
Not C for Czarina, Catherine the Great,
but cute as in Bing Crosby's new wife.
She was pert and saucy
like a pony, the way she swung her hair,
the spit curl pitched like a C
note shining in the apple of her crooner's eye.
My mother gave me
the one name that linked for her
bright bits of charm—
husband and hearth,
three smiling children
and a doll whose string
I could pull
the pacifier ring around her neck,
pull the string
far back from the ivory throat,
hear it snap back
like a slingshot
into the birdsong heart
of the voice box—

hear her call my name.
Was it always only chatter?
It sounds so snowy now
like the black-and-white
TV shows we tried to retrieve
huddled around the Magnavox,
lost, garbled messages
the rabbit ears failed to receive
in the dark, marooned
station of a Saturday night.

Living Proof

1.

Father came home from the Brussels World's Fair
with a doll for my sister and a doll for me.
Halfway around the world he carried
two long boxes,
like a man bringing roses home to his wife.
The crinkling of tissue paper
seemed a faraway sound as Father lifted
the doll and placed her in my arms.
Two yellow braids, coarse as burlap, hung
like ropes I imagined a priest might pull
to bring the good people of a town
to God. My beauty of the cowbells
wore a dress flocked with tiny meadow
flowers and shoes sturdy and pink
like the skin of a cow's udder.
Strung on a wire inside her head,
the marbles of her eyeballs
rattled whenever the lids fell shut,
gravity pulling us both to sleep.
No other girl in Wahiawa
owned such a beauty.
No other girl had a father who had traveled
halfway around the world to bring
his daughter such a beautiful doll.

2.

"The child's anemic.
Look how thin she is.
And tired all the time.
Poor thing!"
Mother sighed.
"Pokanini kid took after me . . ."
Mrs. Matsumoto, listening, puffed
sympathetically on a cigarette.

Mother *was* thin.
And she *was* weaker than Father.
But *anemic* leaked onto the floor,
odorless at first, until you noticed her shivering,
in the corner, the shi-shi girl,
who stood all day in her own puddle,
too shy to raise her own hand.

3.

> *I'm sorry, playmate,*
> *I cannot play with you.*
> *My dolly has the flu.*
> *Boohoo Boohoo Boohoo!*
> *Ain't got no rain barrel.*
> *Ain't got no cellar door.*
> *But we'll be jolly friends,*
> *Forevermore!*

Round and round the yellow sun spun,
round and round like a rickety merry-go-round.
I scratched the record.
The needle hit a rut
in the mud of Boohoo,
a rainy town of sickly children
staring out of windows.
I could not play, stuck inside,
not for the rain but the ache
that chilled my limbs into flames.
Sister took my temperature
with a Popsicle stick,
rationed my cherry-flavored Lifesaver pills,
read my palm, and pronounced
a speedy recovery.
Her walkie-talkie crackled news.
Over and out and she was gone.
A game of marbles,
a bike ride down the lane

sent her into the world
of playmates and jungle warfare.
The *rat-tat-tat!* of hand-to-hand combat
disturbed my rest.
I heard beetles fleeing
out of the leaves, out of nests
they scuttled, running blind.

4.
I'm afraid I have to tell you . . .
I'm afraid I have bad news.
How did the doctor put it
to the young couple he had counseled
through colic, chicken pox, and errant nosebleeds?
He was just a mild-mannered country
doctor used to the common cold.
The sniffles that blew into his office
were not the result of tears.
Halfway around the world it seemed
the drive along winding gullies
to the clinic in the city, a stop
at Scottie's for a milkshake, some fries,
Father lifting me—stiff-jointed,
tender lymph node swollen like a berry—
from the backseat of the car.

5.
Across the street from the clinic
there was a park.
In the center of the park
there was a fountain.
I did not see the water shooting into the air
that day, the water lifting
like someone showering the dusty trees with a hose.
On the other side of the fountain,
through the water and the leaves,
there was a museum,

as grand as any Father had seen in Brussels.
Had we been any other family on an outing
that day, we could have entered the museum,
our footsteps hushed as though
we were entering a cathedral.

6.
Mother served another meal I could not
eat, roast beef, mashed potatoes, frozen peas.
She did not say "Put some meat on your bones."
She did not say anything.
I could not reach for the fork.
I could not eat, and feared
she did not expect me to, stuck in a body
that was failing me, ticking ticking
loudly like Mother's kitchen timer or Sister's metronome,
making us all jumpy.
In the mud of Boohoo,
there was a church and a steeple
and if you opened your hands
you could see all the good people.
Somewhere along the equator
far from that town,
there was the marrow,
a place I imagined buried deep inside me
where birds no longer came to drink at the fountain.

7.
Father on his knees
acted as a man who had already surrendered.
On a trip back from the city,
one he thought would be our last,
he stopped at Sears Roebuck
and carried me from the car.
Sleigh ride songs and the chilly
blast of air-conditioning
piped cold as intravenous through my veins.

I looked up at the multitude—
shelves of dolls floating toward the ceiling.
No coarse braids held them down
like heavy rope.
No cowhide shoes to get stuck in the mud.
Father kneeled beside me.
His hands held a voice,
wingless and trapped.
"You can have whichever one you want."
The dolls shimmered in cellophane,
glistened in their dresses of ice.
I looked at him, confused.
Christmas was a month away.
If I chose to go with an angel,
then I would be one too.
Outside, far from the cold air,
rain washed the dust from the trees.
I shook my head and refused.
The birds were flying home.

The Child Floats in a Sea of Grass

The universe regards her,
holds her
resplendent
in suspension.

The child floats in a sea of grass
and one day
asks
how old is the god.

The sky of her mind
now spinning,
again the child
asks

how old is the god,
asks and is
no longer
utterly free.

The mortal mother,
confined to a mirror
like a room of shutters
that once fluttered open,

does not answer.

The eye spins inward,
meaningless as glass,
meaningless as marble,
meaningless as paperweight.

The planet drifts,
orbiting
its own
socket.

The flesh,
contracting into a pinpoint
light of pain,
presses nails into palms,

digs faith into dirt—
nicks that tally up the years,
little rungs
on a lifeline of devotion.

Prayers in the pocket,
a boat,
a cross,
a ladder.

Does it matter—

How old is the god.

The child floats in a sea of grass.

The universe regards her,
holds her
resplendent in its own
invention.

What Is Given

The body's life is a mechanical life—
death built in, and desire.
Cells age, replenish, age and expire.
Everywhere, desire is plentiful; aging is earnest.

The boy at sixteen is dying as surely as he is at sixty,
fulfilling his death path entered the moment the body
took up the tumor of his life, an orderly
mathematics of cellular division, finite and given.

Against the simple complexity the mind
shouts, wanting out of the eat, piss, sleep & sex
built into the death
of it, the wall of skin, the years allowed.

Agitator, destroyer of peace, the mind
with its will, its own immensity presses
thought through the complacent as-it-is-ness,
a shapeless bristling, this thinking intensity.

Holder of grudges, expounding worry,
the mind's faulty mechanism is unforgiving.
Thinking thinking thinking, it shakes sleep to pin something
down, pounds its nails, aimless and divergent.

Arms that carved an ocean, lungs that swallowed air
would resolve into the physical
were it not for the mind that struggles,
measuring loss against what was always settled, finite, and given.

Fetters

Every morning I come to Shoshinge.
Every morning it is the same.

Between my mind and the mind of compassion,
Amida Buddha's wisdom and light,
the hymn flutters like a veil.
All is settled.
All is well.

I am the recipient of all that is settled,
of all that is well.
I long to enter the veil.
I give up my voice,
coarse, thick phlegm stone of sleep,
to meet the infinite
bountifulness with breath
moments of faith.
Every morning it is the same.
All is settled.
All is well.
I long to enter the veil.

I open my mouth, a cave
blackened with the smoke of desire.
I open my throat to lift
stone from breath and push
what falls firm
in the heavy tide of night.

My sorrowing heart staggers into sunlight
drunk with complaints,
easily distracted,
burdened and unsettled.
It wails.

Sing, praise, surrender!
All is assured
but my heart, blindfolded, attaches
disappointments, pins grievances
upon the veil like a child
spinning in circles, left
holding the donkey's tail.

I fling my worries upon the veil,
a tangled web of fetters.
Cluttered heart!
So disorderly and rude!

Every morning I come to Shoshinge.
Every morning it is the same.

The Roses of Guadalajara

Oh you tireless watcher!
What have I done to you?
That you make everything I dread
and everything I fear come true?

  —Joni Mitchell

She Meant to See China

She meant to see China as if China were an old rerun
she could always catch at the Princess Theater,
a matinee she may have wandered into as a child
in the only picture I have of my mother from that time.

Nine years old,
squinting into the sun,
she stands straight, her back to a wall.

She meant to see China with her two daughters,
ride a riverboat past ink-washed mountains,
the long braids of her daughters' hair
whipping like banners in the wind.

She stands against a wall,
hair cut
neat and practical,
chopped blunt as a boy's
as if the amateur barber knew
haircuts for this child were few.

She meant to see China with her two daughters,
visit the flickering shrine of an ancestral village,
knock on the door of a distant relative,
see the resemblance.

Mug shot pose, so serious, thin
shift of a dress, thin bare arms,
she stands, her back to a wall.
Motherless, Fatherless,
she squints into the sun.

She meant to see China,
walk the great structures,
the dragon tail of the longest one
visible from the moon.

Who cut my mother's hair?
Who sat her on the crate and draped
a cloth across her shoulders?
Who told her to sit still
even though a warm wind blew
hair into her mouth, hair
stiff as the burnt offerings of joss sticks,
hair that blew into my mother's mouth?

She meant to see China with her two daughters,
ride a riverboat,
walk the Great Wall,
take a picture of some old resemblance,
pay her respects.

Someone swept the black leavings
off the back porch.
A warm wind blew the burnt sticks
across the lane of feed stores, butcher shops,
soda fountains, tiny dwellings, temple bells,
sounds of orphans, derelicts, philanthropists
and angels
ringing in that tiny bell.

She meant to see China,
buy velvet slippers, the ones that make no sound,
bring back to School Street a suitcase full of red ones,
red and beaded, swirling with dragons.

Someone cut my mother's hair,
dusted behind the ears,
shooed the child into the street,
pressed into her hand
a fortune
so she could catch the movie,
buy something to eat.

An extravagant sum,
a warm steamed bun.

My mother clanked down the long stairs of the wooden
walk-up
visible from the moon.

Someone mumbled a prayer.

Someone threw in
the sweet sour reminder,
Good daughter,
Take care.

The Valley Boat

I lost my mother once
to sadness,
but she returned
and I became her daughter again.
My family and I rejoiced at the sound
of her laughter in the kitchen.
The broth grew strength
from the oxtail,
a gold rim of fat
lining our stomachs.
We thought we could hide
in the shelter of her laughter forever.
When sadness rained
a year later,
I knew before she did
that she was going away,
that she would be leaving
us and all
we could do
was make her comfortable,
ease the passage
back into the dark
waters of herself
as if we were preparing
a boat up a slow, sad river,
provisioned with the flowers
and fruits
that she could remember us by
so she could find her way
as she did the first time,

find her way home
to the house of happiness
and good fortune
that she had built
in the years before she had to leave.

Stone Soup

The child grieves for the mother
as a mother grieves for a child,
and in the woolen smoke of that grief
wound like a muffler
around a chimney's thin neck,
illness breathes windswept words
across the soup, now cold,
inedible potatoes
harsh as stones.

Committed

Committed she was to rage
as another might have been to art,
a commitment
she knitted night after night.
Busy hands kept her secret.
Knots of grievances
thorned a fence
around her heart.
A suit of armor,
chain-linked,
she donned one day,
ready for battle.
The unsuspecting beast in us all slept,
awakened we were by the wild
torch of her tongue.
It scorched our good intentions,
what had kept her
locked all those
years in a tower
without
a way out—no rope of hair,
she ranted, no queen-size chair,
she shouted, not even
a shred of something
decent to wear.
God knows,
the litany rang,
what she had to do
without.

The Expense of Mildew

Mildew is expensive to keep
off the tiles of the Roman pool, requiring
a midnight shift of scrubbers whose work
Mother understands is a hidden cost,
difficult to calculate
when no actual cash changes hands, just a jaded
scribbling my sister manages as she leads
Mother through glass doors to the inner
sanctum of lockers.
We exchange our street clothes
for white robes and clear plastic slippers
made in Italy.

We are her attendants, leaving the efficient ones
to lift the white robes off the shoulders of the young
Japanese women composed as statues.
They drape themselves around the Roman pool
and drink green tea iced like the washcloths
they press to close cleansed pores.
Expectations are flawlessly met as a foot
extended into the perfect water.
They have worked hard for this beauty package,
these office girls who in another country
shuffle paper anonymously, shuffle
their hidden bodies into crowded trains
stuffed with the breath of humanity.
Having arrived at the coastal spa,
they enter the extravagance of mist,
moisture gift wrapped,
without stepping into the scorched air,
without damage done to skin
as unblemished as the well-scrubbed grout between the tiles.

Two weeks ago Mother's lungs collapsed.
She turned blue without breath until
Father exchanged his air for emptiness,

kept filling her lungs with his haggard breath
until a machine stabilized her breathing
and breathed for her.
Breathed her back into life, a more or less
comfortable sleep.
At four in the morning Father summoned
his daughters to be at her side.
When Mother awoke she had nothing to report to us.
There was no news of the afterlife, just a timid
intake of air
that kissed her into the same oblivion
she had been living all her life.

The eucalyptus mist is expensive
and so is the water, therapeutically salted
to a perfection beyond the ocean's own briny composition
boiling off the rocks on the other side
of the artificial lagoon.

We are her attendants, we will take her
as far as she is comfortable. Her body remains
hidden in a bathing suit. We will not see
Mother naked, not this time, only the raw
hands that scrubbed mildew off bathroom walls
until nails chipped and knuckles thickened.
We release her into the swirling water.
Anxiety splashes against her face.
The mist arising out of the steamy pool,
leaking out of the steamy sauna,
is heavy like smoke.
She coughs, unable to relax and enjoy herself
for lodging in her lungs like phlegm
is the worry that is always there,
the hidden cost of everything,
mildew appearing on the breathwing of spores.

Fragrance Is the First to Go

Fragrance is the first
to go but color clings its rust
to petals tightly clustered as a fist of feathers.
How many roses I have hung
by stem to bleed a little longer.
Upside down in bunches
they hang, throats slit, like chickens
held until the last drop
gushes into dirt.
Set the bird upon the ground
and it will run,
not knowing it is already dead.
My roses I bleed to death,
the last drop choking the body of the rose—
petals shrunken, used up, already dead.
Fragrance is the first
to go and the body crumbles soon after,
petals unable to hold
the will, the surge, the rush
of pigment pulsing blooms into dust.

Rust

By the bridge
near their apartment
my parents pause to sip the tea light
of late afternoon, the soiled air
a communion of dust and light
slanting through the white buildings.
A glass elevator delivered them
from the ninth floor, a journey
in a time capsule
that ends in a picture they will not frame—
one in which they are very old,
one in which something else was promised,
not this, my mother's depression and
the resulting astonishing compression of years.
It has taken my mother her
feet, one foot in front of the other,
a dull hour's work
and my father's steady arm
to walk the fifty yards to the water's
edge.
Across the water
cars stream in one direction,
fueled by the expletive
horns and gestures,
then disperse at the point
where the canal disgorges its lot into the sea.
Tilapia congest the thick
green waters, lapping
the undergrowth of shadows.
The black sponge bodies swell like tongues
exposed to salt, wind, and sun.
What a day overspent at the beach
would do to my child's skin,
as my mother discovered in a naked stall
peeling back like a Band-Aid

the thin straps of my swimsuit
to gasp at the striped flesh
crisp as rock-salted shrimp.
Don't speak to her about overexposure—
rust and the corrosive power of elements—
the internal ones
that drought the brain
from inside out,
the clashing cymbals of alloys,
odd metals, my mother's curious melting point.
The leak occurred over the years
like an imperceptible incontinence,
the faucet drip no one in the house heard,
the loss of precious fluids, something vital missing.
She rattles about inside
the hollow husk of her body—
a dead seed,
the fluorescent pill, the sentimental
tooth the fairy never took because my mother
in the end was the good fairy—
a noisemaker that doesn't make any noise.
She turns and tugs at my father's sleeve
in this rock bottom layer of shadows.
Take me home, she rasps,
as if to say enough
of air, I've had enough
of it to drink.

Horizon

Space unrelieved terrifies.
We worship what we do not see.
A child adds a tree, a sun—solar
flower maned with fire petals, a roof
pitched to break
a field of sky,
polka dots of clouds to decorate
an idea of heaven.
Blank heaven needs our adornment.
Ideas, humble encasements, sent up in thought,
thin as balloon skins,
frail and weak.
While earth, poor dirt of earth
we plow pull weeds plant feet
is given a meager line—
truest gesture of our terror—
this line drawn
grim as a mouth, set firm,
locked without teeth.

Riverbed

When she was ill,
my mother's feet
appeared to be the injured ones,
never mind the illness
in her head
that dragged her down into
the quicksand of her sixty-five-year-old
body. The whole
anatomy of the foot,
both left and right,
twisted into the talons
of some great bird
gripping something
none of us knew.
In the afternoons
I'd come upstairs to her room
where she lay
eyes closed, fully awake,
her feet, a pair on pillows,
nesting like shards dredged from a T'ang riverbed.
I'd take each foot, one foot
at a time, into my hands,
try to unburden that rigid claw
set like a jaw wired shut.
I could have broken
the delicate arch
for all the pressure I exerted
to release the tension of those
feet clutching an invisible perch,
but under solemn interrogation
each foot remained steadfastly silent,
beyond cure,
as if conspiring to confound
those who would try
with love's arrogance
to ease even a portion of pain.

Peacefully, on the Wings of Forgiveness

A man takes into his hands
his wife's injured foot,
gnarled as a gingerroot by years of wearing
the wrong shoes,
poor-grade cowhide from Brazil,
fictive leather's friction of cardboard
lacking proper arch supports.
Her foot has sustained incompatible twists and strains,
the scrimping steps that lead to numbness.
Her foot drops limp, an appendage
she drags like a rice sack, unable to keep
up with where her mind wants to go.
Yesterday he would have scolded her
for walking around town without feeling
the pus boiling yellow under the toe.
Iodine rusts a square of cotton.
The man prepares a swab to muffle the infection.
She waits to dodge
the arrows of accusation.
How is it possible
you couldn't feel anything?
But today forgiveness plucks the sting
out of the man's heart,
as if it were a splinter, a thorn, or a glass shard
whose removal allows a tiny bloom
to fill the puncture.
Forgiveness softens his face
into the one he carried to the woman
across the years
unruffled by the wind of worry,
when there was no history between them to erase.
The man who once crossed the dance floor of the gymnasium,
polished as a mirror's lake,
takes her foot as tenderly as he once took her hand.
And in taking it, he lifts himself into motion.

He remembers the pleasure of her lightness—
shining across the water—
the beautiful girl who ate nothing for a week
in order to buy some shoes.

Blue

Blue is the silence she sinks into,
the spiraling down
of a shell
whorling
through layers of receding sound.
Laughter at the kitchen table,
bobbing like little girls moored to pink mermaid rings,
dims the way trinket lights
in a seaside town
blink out, leaving in darkness
those who drift toward night.
Haven't we heard by now?
The world is no longer round.
It lies flat like the table
we sit around and break open
the pearls of rice.
We think to entice her tongue
to articulate ancient speech,
the clicking of chopsticks,
the slurping of seaweed soup.
Hunger's tentacles are not powerful enough
to pull her out of the blue.
She sits at the edge of that deep
blue where talk falls asleep
in her hands.
Hot potato!
I want to yell
but the words sit there in her lap,
diffused.
She is already floating on her back.
She rides the tide of sadness,
blue veiling her like the bride
she once was,
then as now, forever
willing to be taken
by surprise.

The Roses of Guadalajara

Nights on the *Regent Star*, my father walked
the plank with my mother, her arm cradled
like a cripple in his, he led her through
conversations she felt ill-at-ease with, meals
at the captain's table, wandered through
the eyes which had no appetite, no desire
for the passport pleasures of the Panama Canal,
Puerto Vallarta, vendors yelling yellow trinkets
of straw hats and papier-mâché animals,
turquoise-painted wooden boxes her five granddaughters
might have treasured as some token of her presence,
as did her daughters twenty-five years ago in Guadalajara.

We rode a carriage through a garden of roses.
Bees wreathed a garland of noise
around my mother's head, and she smiled
and waved for the camera, smiled
without her lips, without her body, with what appears
to be now the beginning of her sadness.

We rode a carriage through a garden of roses,
the summer roses of the dusty city, around the corner,
at every plaza a fountain of roses, pink
roses, red roses, yellow roses spilling
a withering sweetness.

I bought a box painted with blue roses
in the mercado one afternoon when the carriage
stopped. Too hot to think, the noise, the flies,
the tanned hides, warm Coca-Cola in cool
green bottles, past the embroidered blouses—
more roses, thick, crested mounds of roses
on collars and bodices, satin-stitched in a manic
profusion of threads too heavy for the poor
muslin sagging under the weight of the roses.

I've kept the box for twenty-five years.
Nothing in it, nothing in it but a few buttons,
a donkey pin, a glass swallow from Capistrano,
a baby's tooth—which child's?—a morsel of umbilical
cord—which child's?—desiccated as a tongue of beef jerky.
I bought a box smothered with blue roses.
And why she slept my father tore at her silence—
Look—there's Acapulco. Look at it! You'll never
see it again—the *Regent Star* sails into a night
of a day, so many roses she can't remember.

I bought a box, a nesting box, a box
painted with blue roses, singing birds, and filigreed leaves.

White Ashes

Better I was carried from the womb
straight to the grave.
I see the diggers waiting,
they're leaning on their spades.
  —Joni Mitchell

Mountains of Ash

Stark tree of the clothesline
shivers as we pull wind-dried
sheets from the pinch of wooden claws.

Time to bring in the laundry.
Time to come inside.

Evening rises cool to citrus,
pomelo, lemon, and tangerine hanging low, almost
touching the ground.

Although it is chilly,
Grandpa chooses to stay outside.
He stands like a totem in a circle of clay pots
stacked beside old shoes, old hats.

Skillful in discerning rubble from stone,
tattered fishing net from useful orchid screen,
our eyes scan mercilessly,
until we feel
our work is done.

When we finish emptying the smallest
heart nesting inside a shoe box
Grandma hid under the bed,
we begin again,
fanning out to comb the yard
as Grandpa in another life once trimmed bonsai.
There's always that stray tug leaf hair twig
we miss in that first go around.

Two friends descend into the smallest
heart-shaped boxes of a house—
hairpins, paper clips, cuff links, foreign coins,

dim photographs the size of postage stamps—
deciding what the dying need
to save in order to live
after the dead have come and gone.

Still, we know the house holds more.

No one bothers to answer
and Grandpa nods and unplugs his hearing
aid, keeps an eye on our work
of emptying carrying hauling thirty forty fifty
bags now piled outside the door.

Still, we know the house holds more.

"What about the fleas?"
Grandma asks every visitor.
"Has anyone seen the fleas?"

News of his wife in the nursing home
reaches through the static.
"She plays bingo, Grandpa."
"Her nails are painted pink."
"She thinks she's on an ocean liner."

Without the whining and the pissing,
Grandpa sleeps better.

"When will I see her?"
he asks.
Dog or wife, no one bothered to answer.

We grab the piss-drenched sheets
chased like bad dreams into corners.
Blame it on the dog.

Piss-drenched sheets
stuffed into pillowcases
reveal Grandma's distressing clarity.

The day they came for Grandma
she was standing by the stove,
weeping at the boiling water.

Neglect is an odor ammonia can't scrub out.
It seeps its soot into linoleum,
blooms a violent flower across the mattress.

An avalanche awaits us.
Pennies empty drawers.
Comic books sift through fingers.
Valentines and crossword puzzles
break the feeble string of boxes.

How many pencils did a family need?
We rubberband in bunches the pencils—
yellow arrows, stiff petal-less daffodils.

Debris emptying an interior
weighs more than grass and leaves.

Down the stairs and out the door, and still,
the house holds more.

The moths have eaten the dresses.
Dust
of the last feast
fills pockets, sleeves.
No use for trophies,
Elroy drives a taxi with no particular address,
with no particular direction
except the next grubby fare.
Kyle, tender even then,

honks the rented truck to haul
what we begin in the morning
to carry out of the house.

Grandma fed us fists of rice
packed hard as snowballs,
musubi we saved for the drive-in movie,
a broken fence our ticket through.
By the time the lights went out
we had reached the tiny plum.
We sucked on the salt of it
until our tongues
shrank small and thirsty in our mouths.

We slid back into darkness and gazed up.
Snow fell across the screen—
snow falling and people talking
in voices we strained to hear.
No car to hook the speaker to.
The luminous screen lit the neighborhood.

Tin star of Keiko's window
nailed to the night.

We slid back into darkness and gazed up.

In another life Keiko and I slept
upon a futon light as a morning cloud.

Grandpa's prayers perfumed my dreams.
Even then I knew he was wise. Even then.

I smell the soap of a morning's shave,
brush my face against the stubble he's missed.

When we descend he climbs the stairs
to the altar, a converted closet,
slacks and shirts cast aside for Odaishisama.

Sennenko blackens the cave of his room.
He prays for the dead and the dying,
mostly he prays for the dying.
His prayers form a mountain of ash.

The psyche cannot move until
the house is put in order.

Enough years have passed to place
a mother's sweaters in a bin marked charity.

The mother of Katherine,
the mother of Keiko.
Three generations of women
in a two-story house.

The blood ran through the women.
They kept water in the kettle,
a flame on the stove.
They kept the men coming back to the table.

Without a wife to attach him as in-law,
Katherine's husband found himself
an outlaw in a house too small.

Blame it on the dog.

In another life there was Katherine—
someone's wife, someone's mother, someone's daughter
who kept things going
with her laughter, hula lessons, bowls of gardenia
in every room.

"Has anyone seen the fleas?"

He found himself an outlaw in a house too small,
crumbs wedged between stove and sink.
Find him
the cup of tea that vanished.

Find him.

Dying is what we do, and do
so well we weep and drink and let
things fall into cracks.

"When will I see her?"

Bowls of gardenia, luminous
bowls of water.

In another life there was Katherine.

We ate the rice
to reach the gem
of the plum,
the salty salty plum.

How many pencils did a family need?

Keiko returns to dig from under
those buried there.

Grandpa stands like a totem.
His prayers form a mountain of ash.

Time to bring in the laundry.
Time to come inside.

Best friends since childhood, we return
to put the house to rest.

Tin star of Keiko's window,
silver pin on a mother's dress.

Two friends descend upon a neglected house.
An avalanche awaits us.

There are pencils enough to keep
the schoolchildren of a small country happy.

A Poet in the House

Emily's job was to think.
She was the only one of us
who had that to do.
    —*Lavinia Dickinson*

Seemingly small her work,
minute to the point of invisibility—
she vanished daily into paper, famished,
hungry for her next encounter—
but she opened with a string of humble
words necessity,
necessary as the humble work
of bringing well to water, roast to knife, cake to frost,
the coarse, loud, grunting labor of the rest of us
who complained not at all
for the noises she heard
we deemed divine, if
claustrophobic and esoteric—
and contented ourselves to the apparent,
the menial, set our heads
to the task of daily maintenance,
the simple order at the kitchen table,
while she struggled with a different thing—
the pressure seized upon her mind—
we could ourselves not bear such strain
and, in gratitude, heaved the bucket,
squeezed the rag, breathed the sweet,
homely odor of soap.
Lifting dirt from the floor
I swear
we could hear her thinking.

Book of Hours

What led you to the book
and kept you there
was pleasure, a simple
stirring—unconditional.

The function of spelling,
the mechanics of handwriting
fed an orderly compulsion, repetitive
acts as tight as stitches—
a balm for inner disruption.

Pure to the task of setting
letters in a row, filigreed nonsense
curved extravagant and slow.
Intent on making O just so,
sound connected on air's blue note.
Meaning broke, lifted: sky poured in.
The hand's enactment of the mind's enchantment.
The letters illuminated—glowed.

Hours spent in odd posture,
girl with head bent, her hair a scrawl.
Who knows where she went,
hanging letters on pale blue lines—
hook of star,
tiny magnificent clothes,
adornments to an original country.

Blueroses

Nine is the age at which girls left their mothers and entered the
service of Artemis, the virgin huntress who resembled a boy in
her strength and wildness.
> —*Emily Hancock,* The Girl Within

Blueroses showed up the summer
I turned nine, the summer
when left to my own devices
I fell into a crevice of neglect.
A state of mind I suspect
for Blueroses to arrive at my doorstep.
I slid manic into midnight
where Blueroses backstroked beyond the net of curfew.
I heard the splashing of the lake
tracing a curlicue's mad logic
after the smoke from backyard barbecues had fed
those who waited for the goodnight kiss on clean white
    foreheads.
She held her breath
and I descended.
She appeared to woo me to myself,
a vow she took to break
the spell of spinners
sleepwalking toward the slumbering veil.
Blueroses gave me thorns—
you'll need them—she whispered—
a loud horn—
and this too—she whispered—
a petal torn from her sleeve.
Blueroses retrieved me out of the long
blue hours spent pitching stones
into the late afternoons of a lake,
pulled me into the blue body of water
where my body, intact, solitary unto itself,
awakened on a sea of blue-stitched roses.

She thread me through her eye
and stitched for me
invisibility.
She pulled me through my mind.
I disappeared into myself,
the solitary act of entering
a work of art.
She cleared her throat
when I sharpened my pencil,
sang when I pressed
the pointed lead into the skin of paper,
prepared myself to bleed for her.
Once awakened I longed for the breath
she breathed through the window, my body
rising to the petals borne across
the blue distances of roses.
Impatient with dusting,
I fell through the cracks of the random
inspections of the absentminded ones
who had yet to count me among the missing—
the idle, yes—
a small heap of bones
to be one day sewn
into something useful.
Blueroses breathed patience into my hands
when music mattered,
not the imitation dusting
but the polishing of the roses,
slowing down my hands to stitch
the minutes of practice
into seamless time,
tranquil as petals.
Left to our own devices,
we flourished.
Left to our own capable invention,

I breathed the blue possibility of roses
to mirror myself
in a thousand stitches
a thousand petals
a thousand strokes
across the blue distances
recited with the pleasurable ease of swimmers.

I made myself too visible.
I made pleasure in my own time apparent.
I could not hide my happiness.
My name was among the spoken—
isn't it time to reclaim our daughter,
isn't it time to tame her—
and the blue distances were broken,
all those roses that were within my breath to give.
I watched myself
answer the call home to supper—
the children are hungry,
the men are waiting to be fed.
I watched myself turn from the water,
tie on the saddle shoes,
and receive the blessings of servitude.
I entered the long line of spinners.

A splash, a cry—
just a few more breaths across the water!—
and Blueroses,
disappearing into the place
where I last saw her,
entered the moment
like a bookmark,
a petal pressed between the torn years
I kept turning page after page in the dark.

The Sister

The boy did not know the girl had a sister.
This was to cause him great confusion. Years later
he would still wonder which one he had truly possessed.
He chose to turn his ear to the voice of the quietest singing,
a kind of singing the boy himself had known
when he dug the deepest hole in the darkest part of the night.
The voice he thought he heard changed color
at the moment the girl became aware of the boy's intelligent ears.

The boy knew about the loneliness of men.
His father had died of it.
His mother despised it.
She sent the boy to live with his brother.
The boy's brother was also lonely.
The boy knew this about his brother.

One day the boy found something in his brother's drawer
that made him feel lonelier than he had ever felt before.
More lonely than the time his mother had punished him
for fucking her boss's fourteen-year-old daughter.
Maggie—that was her name—cried and cried.
His mother sprayed him with the backyard hose,
threw him out, and returned to answering the phone for Maggie's father.
She threw a blanket and a pillow into the dead dog's house
and told him to go and live like the dog that he was.
Something about *No son of mine.*
She tossed a bone for effect. The bone nicked his cheek.
A scar grew out of her anger.

Hidden under the mismatched socks the boy found a wad of tinfoil.
Of course he opened it, peeling back the petals to find inside a silk panty.
The boy sniffed it. His erection was instantaneous.

It became apparent to the boy that his brother
sniffed it often—and between the two of them sneaking into

the flower for a quick sniff, the panty began to lose its scent.
The boy, afraid his brother would send him back to their mother,
tried sprinkling the crotch with water as if a little moisture
would resurrect out of the pinch of crust the scent of a girl
his brother had once known.

The boy could not ask his brother about such things.
They were two lonely men living in two separate rooms
of a poorly ventilated rented house.

Maggie's voice was clear and light
like her eyes that took in nothing that would darken them.
Even when she cried, the boy sensed
she was acting outside herself.

One night Maggie showed up at his doghouse drunk.
The boy had a hard time explaining his lack of desire.
He said *exile*. He said *banishment*. She laughed,
unhooked her bra, and told him not to be so *serious*.
That's when he said *fleas, no room,* and *mother.*
Maggie forgot her shoes as she hurried away.
He wondered what to do with her shoes.
She was always hurrying away after that.
He figured she was trying to forget she had ever left them
outside the doghouse.
Forget the strawberry-nippled breasts jiggling toward his mouth.
She looked like a girl who had plenty of shoes.

He hung the shoes from the ceiling of the doghouse.
They gave him something to look at,
a mobile of thin buckles, straps, and heels.
He would stare at them and think of all the places
he and Maggie would never see.

The boy was ready to go anywhere when his mother sent him to live
with his brother. His mother was tired of trying
not to think of him living in the doghouse.

She told him to come back inside.
He refused.
He had staked a corner of the yard as his own.
She felt his eyes on her whenever she settled in for an evening
of television. She stopped drawing the drapes.
She carried the television into her room.
She erected rabbit ears.
And although she felt safe she could never fully enjoy
the jar of pistachio nuts she kept beside her bed.

The boy listened a long time to the voice of the quietest singing
long after he had chased it away by his attention.
He could hear the full possession the voice inhabited.
A voice that was not afraid of the dark.
He turned his ear to the welling that snagged every truth
dragged out of the body's deceit, full bodied, ragged as
the smoke and the kisses that would be taken joyfully into the body.

The girl liked the way the boy lingered after the bell rang,
the edge of his shadow touching hers.
When his circling brought him to stand beside her,
they were surprised to find she was taller.
The fur on the boy's arms stiffened.
He caught a whiff of the other dwelling.

The voice of the quietest singing pulled on the girl
who strained to the point of snapping in anger
and breaking the chain of flowers pieced together—
shells gathered, sandwiches shared—
the companionable stitches of their life intact.
The feud raged within herself.
The girl did not want to be reminded of her duty to stay close to the pack.
She was tired of swimming the same waters,
tired of days spent alone with her own kind.
The voice of the quietest singing retreated as if wounded,
and hid.
The boy remained alert, ready to offer his heart.

The boy began to follow her home
every day after school, at a distance,
a distance his bowels registered with fear
as he approached the girl's street.
It could have been Maggie's neighborhood the way he saw himself
as a trespasser. The houses smelled of mothers who stayed at home,
of clean-shaven fathers who hired women like his mother
to answer their phones.
He felt his words would shatter through his teeth
and make her hurry away.
He could not believe she would find his devotion
good enough.

The voice of the quietest singing cooked for the father,
ironed the newspaper after reading the horoscope
so that when the father came home from work—
a signal to turn off the radio—the newspaper
was as fresh as if it had just been delivered.
The boy, his shadow touching the edge of the patio, watched
through the screen door the evenings
the girl ate quietly beside the father who did not need to speak to his daughter.
The sound of the chopsticks clicking the air between them
made the boy feel like howling out of that deep hole.

Dreams about the boy the girl was having
made her glad she and her father rarely spoke.
The girl sang recklessly now.
The boy's proximity required this.
The girl wanted to spoil the boy.
She wanted to feed him treats sneaked out of her father's house.
She wanted to give him a good washing, especially
behind the ears. She wanted to stroke his wild hair.
The boy, crouching in the flaming croton, howled.

One night the boy ventured closer.
The girl's dog barked, rattling its chain so loudly
the boy ditched into a hedge.

The dog kept barking, the chain kept rattling.
A light blinked on in a window.
The girl appeared and saw the boy crouching in the flaming croton.
She tapped the glass.
My father is not home.
The boy bounded toward the door, careful
to avoid the dog straining the chain
to the point of snapping its puny neck.
The girl slipped open the latch,
the dog howled,
and the boy sprang at her.
The girl fell back onto the living room floor
and let herself be covered with kisses.

The voice of the quietest singing said nothing to the father.
She cooked his meals, set aside the newspaper—she no longer
read her horoscope—clicked the chopsticks like knitting needles,
keeping worry to herself. She could no longer be
the guardian to herself.
In this way she remained in hiding.
In this way she lived two lives.
The nights found her running to meet the boy in the spot
they had carved, a diamond in the middle of the baseball field.
She ran to be knocked down on the pitcher's mound,
to feel with each kiss pressing down into her body
a shooting star.
The boy, so hungry with his kisses, lost his way.
The girl became frightened by the loneliness that entered her body.
The boy mistook silence for the quiet singing, so quiet now
he had to dig deeper to hear any sound.

The burden of a baby brought the voice out of hiding.
It brought her forward to speak to the father,
who rushed into his daughter's room and tore from the walls
every picture, tore from the shelves
every book, tore from the bureau
every flower from its glass vase, every jewel

from its silken drawstring pouch.
The voice of the quietest singing came out of the shadows,
came out of hiding to console the father.
The girl traced "La Vie en Rose" in the tiny figure
of a ballerina twirling across the mirror.
Before the figure reached the other side of the lake,
a hand shut the lid on the music.

Banishment Exile No daughter of mine Don't you ever speak to her again
The words broke through the boy's skull.

Sometimes at night the voice of the quietest singing
stands at the window and senses
he is out there, crouched in the flaming croton,
a boy looking in at a family that would try to forget
the disturbance, the fact that hunger and loneliness
had ever visited, or indeed, had ever existed.

Honored Guest

Use the muse that threatens to devour.
Use the muse to break desire.
Muse of joy, muse of grief,
both speak enchantment differently.
One whispers body, one shatters mind.
Both spell afflictions extreme.
One burns the body with the sigh of longing,
gently disruptive, a mild opiate
willingly called.
Gentle wind you attach
yearning to someone
seen once long ago.
Conjuring is sweet, tender, and restrained.
Impossibility makes it so.

It's the other disruptive power of another
who has your number,
who calls you on the phone to discuss
superfluous matter, reckless unending drama
of its own mind.
This is the shattering one, a wild stimulant
unwittingly called.
Once engaged, it wants in,
intimacy unearned—and for you,
a thousand fires.
This dangerous maker of curses
and serious chatter
strickens you, renders
you flat.
Master of distraction,
it likes you like that.
Unable to spell,
you are unable to sing.

Use the muse that threatens to devour.
Use the muse of desire
to break the struggle into matchsticks
for your own secret fire.
You be maker, expert speller.
Cast the poem, count each significant letter.
Shake the crazy laughter of its rattle.
Dry seeds scatter, diffused.
Use the muse that threatens to devour.
Use it.
Invite into your well-made home
antagonist as most anticipated guest.

In the Far Wing of an Old Museum

> They come to *feel* pictures, to seek mood,
> color, or a shape that evokes in them
> an inner passion, a completion of self.
> They respect silence and privacy, and their
> alliance is acknowledged with only the slightest
> nod or glint of eye contact. They snort or groan—
> few words are spoken. They usually travel alone.
> —*Wakako Yamauchi*

In the drizzle of rain
we may have met
as travelers even then
when we had time
to wander into art
some odd and dormant
years ago the curtain of day
collapsing into the eclipse
the black umbrellas dripped
at the closing hour of an old museum.
Footsteps splashed waves of sound
echoing across cool, tiled pools of marble,
carrying us to another shore
where paintings scrolled into rivers
we came to bathe in,
dipping our gaze into ancient light
as if to recover
the receding moments
we lose to the seamless one
the way a stone disappears
by first disturbing
the lake's still surface.
The face that pressed the moment's
passing your face—a pair of hands
and eyes expressing
joy—was one we both possessed,
singular in the apprehension

at the perfection
cracked
into a thousand-year-old
vase,
delicate as a teacup,
porcelain-lipped
like the waterlilies outside pouring rain.

A City of Sleeves

Even the brushing of sleeves between passersby
reveals a deep connection in past lives.
   —*Japanese saying*

Sleeves brush, touch, and fall away

A city of sleeves brushing, touching, and falling away

A city of sleeves sleeps and breathes

White sleeves of mourning
Black sleeves of grief
Old sleeves of regret
Blue sleeves asleep on a train

A city of sleeves
Burning leaves

Red sleeves of desire
The speed with which we are traveling

Lights along the river

Tickets, transits, stations
Exits, entrances, hesitations

A procession of lights and floating windows
Discrete as cutlery

Ashtrays, fountain pens, paperweight
Of the bluest glass
Elbows on the table

A city of sleeves dreaming
This life tolerable

The brushing of sleeves between strangers
Between travelers
Between us

Torn, ragged, black and blue

Blue sleeves of a young man asleep on a train

He is as real to you as any longing
An appointment you did not mean to keep
But kept

Arriving
Time tunneling its train of twilight and wet black leaves
The smell of smoke and wood

Night's row of impenetrable hedges, shoulders, everywhere
Thick black hair

Such appearances remain hidden
Until such time
The brushing of sleeves

Becomes suddenly personal
A bridge we cross as we rushed to greet
Our happiness

Unscrolling
Sleeves of dreams
A room without pillows
Defining the gesture of our hands

A young man riding a twilight train

In the city of leaves he was a stark
Feature of your dreams

The child you gave up
When you yourself were a child

Torn, ragged, black and blue

Breath between us

Blue sleeves and an unintelligible arousal

He is as real to you as any longing
Real as the young girl who crossed the river
Weight of the moon blessing her
Sleeves of dreams unfolding
Bountiful, a young girl's heart

Blue sleeves brush

Old sleeves of regret
Debts paid, owed, left unsaid

An offering to Jizō of the roadside shrines
Prayers for the unborn child
You carried home in the dark

Water stone child you could not claim in this life

Lying in a room without pillows
Without adornment
Torn, ragged, breath between us

You went as far as you could go
There the earth appeared
Glass blue
Stone wrapped in water

A city of sleeves
Lies between us

Frayed rope of incense
Ringing a soundless bell
Paper wishes tied to a temple tree

Until such time
The brushing of sleeves remains
Breath between us
An empty cup of leaves

Weight of the moon of the bluest glass
The sweetest smoke
The darkest wood

Lights along the river

Black and blue, anonymous
Swirling leaves
A city of sleeves

Until such time
You wait to cross the river

If not in this life
If not

A city sleeps and breathes

Why not love ourselves from this day
Onward

An appointment we keep
In a city of leaves

We will find each other
Say our peace

If not for this life
The singular breath carries us forward

We have eternity
Breath between us

Lights along the river

The speed with which we are travelers

Blue sleeves asleep on a train

The Slow Upheaval of Mist

There is always a man walking down the road, a dog at his side, a man
you saw when you were expecting to see the usual arrangement of trees.
What becomes for you an eternal afternoon came out of the trees'
involvement in the illusion brought in by the slow upheaval of mist.
Uprooted, the trees seemed to float in the air that had turned to water.
You had to begin another logic to understand the appearance of the man
who began to make himself known to you. A man, who by his faithful
recurrence, attaches himself to you, bringing the distance
like a bone for you to examine. Or praise. Or throw out.
You keep the bone, the hard vision of something elusive,
as the man who began at a safe distance circles closer until
he is the one who comes to fix the leak in your roof, positioning
himself to exit and enter unfettered by the cloud of your attention.
You are already beginning to read the pressure
he exerts in his arms as he lifts his body through the skylight.
You think it is another bone tossed into your lap
when you see him in the phone booth at the oddest hour,
when you are wondering why you are driving through rain that batters
your windshield, wondering where in the world you are supposed to be going.
You have difficulty hiding the bone that lies on your pillow
beside your head. It shines and howls and breaks your dreams
into pieces, like the pieces of the house you haul to the dump.
Obstacles splinter, pierce through skin, like the firewood
the man carries in his arms.
He knows you are cold, and in his faithfulness he will see to it
that you have wood. He knows you know how to make a fire.
This knowing agrees with you. He knows you do not know
how to keep the fire from flaming out or burning beyond control.
Coming and going toward each other becomes an act of singleheartedness
taken up by his nature to keep returning
to bring wood that you must split into kindling, the thinnest
possible pencils of bone. The violence done to the heart
of the wood is what builds your house. You knew that when you first
felt the ache he bore upon each nail fastening down
pieces of wood, that ache which builds an illusion.

The Sky-Blue Dress

The light says *hurry* and the woman
gathers the perishables to the table, the fish
thawed to a chilled translucency, the roses
lifted out of a sink of rainwater, the clean hunger
on the faces of her husband and children faithful
as the biscuits they crumble into their mouths.
Hunger is the wedge that keeps them intact,
a star spilling from the fruit
she slices in a dizzying multiplication of hands
wiping a child's mouth of butter, hands
wiping a dishrag across a clean plate.
She stands at the door waving the dishrag—
ready, set, go!—calling the children in, shooing
the children out, caught in a perpetual
dismantling, a restlessness she strikes the rag at
as if she could hush the air invented by flies.

The light says *hurry* and the family
gathers at the table, the tablecloth washed through countless
fumblings of grace, its garland hem of fruits clouds
into blue pools, faded as a bruise or a reckless tattoo or the roses
the woman hurried that morning into the house,
rushing to revive the steaming petals out of wet
bundles of newspaper the roses traveled in
up the mountain from the market by the sea,
flowers more precious than fish
she left spoiling in the backseat of the car.
Petals and flesh are perishable as the starfruit
a friend of the family climbed the tree to save,
tossing to earth what the sun, the birds, the insects
were days, hours, minutes from rotting.
The roses, stems cut at a slant under rainwater,
breathe cool nights into the air thick with biscuits.
On the table beside the roses a dish of butter disappears
as each knife swipes
its portion, its brightness, its wedge of cadmium lemon.

The light says *hurry* and the man
begins to paint roses while his wife tosses in her sleep
and dreams of a dress she wore long before
she was married, a dress that flowed to her feet
when her hair swirled at her knees, swirled
even when she was simply standing under a tree.
The man who was just a boy then remembers
the first time he saw her, she was standing in a river of hair,
remembers this as he begins to paint roses.
She dreams of the sky-blue dress,
how she once filled it with nothing but skin.
Flesh does not fill it.
Neither does wind.
The girl who wore it left it
pinned like a hole in the sky
the woman passes through, sleep
pouring out of her into water,
all the broken water that leaves
the dress empty, simply hanging from a tree.
She throws off the covers and the moon
washes her in a light that is disturbing,
lifts her into a restlessness
that coincides with the appearance of flies
earlier in the week dragging a net of buzzing,
blue and claustrophobic,
forcing her to examine the roses.

The light says *hurry* and the boy
who came to the man and the woman late in marriage
slips his tooth under his parents' pillow.
In this way he knows they will remember to wake up.
He fills the night with his sweet breath,
breath unimpeded, flowing out of the space
once blocked by the tooth.

Behind the rock there is a cave.
Behind the moon there is simply dark space.
His mother will find the tooth when she makes the bed.
She will save it with all the other teeth hidden under pillows—
broken and intact, smooth and milky—
petals and buttons,
slices of the star-shaped fruit,
shells found nesting in the crevice of pools.

Fur

By the shade of fur on his arms
she could tell he had traveled a great distance.
She could tell by the profusion of fur
he was not from around here.
He did not carry the long pole of her brothers
stripped clean of bark.
He did not carry the rust-stained markings on his back.
He carried his odor trapped in his fur,
the scent of the hunted not wet with fear
but vast and wounded
like a gathering of years upon the sea.
And although the flowers hastily plucked from the side of the road
were ordinary, the explosion of petals
releasing pollen, obscuring the road,
was clearly meant for her.

Somewhere a leaf punctured the air, like the bone
of a small animal tearing itself free.

By dawn her brothers would decipher the dirt,
a jagged scrawl limping out of the bushes.
With ash-coated tongues they would lick
the spot where she lifted her face as if to rain.
Her brothers would not think to look for
what they did not expect.
They would not lose the scent
of an odor they never had.
They would not imagine the dust
of flowers feathering her mouth,
only the tongues they owned,
thick pelts gnashing against teeth.

Out of his pouch tumbled a heap of black stones.
The stones glowed cold, the moss
of an echo buried in the tooth of a cave.
The coldness swallowed her.
She could smell the places where he slept,
places where he kept his fur warm.
When he began to pour his breath into his hands,
the stones lit from within
ruby-flamed, the heat of persimmon.
Good sense told her to run but she stepped
deeper to breathe the smoke of his breath
like a spice
unnaming the space between them.

It happened when light fled the forest,
when her brothers stretched string beds between trees
like nets to catch sleep.
It happened on her way home,
all those days of her walking
had with each step brought her home
toward the horizon stretched across a skin of memory.
The sketch of a ship, a shadow really, lifting through:
fur and desire perceived with equanimity.

White Ashes

The body is then sent into an open field
and vanishes from this world
with the smoke of cremation, leaving
only the white ashes.
—*Hakkotsu No Sho*

Borne on the tongue of that first
thin milk,
white ashes sifted through fingers pinching
fields into crust.
Kitchen mathematics and the pleasure of pie tins
diverted an accordion
fan of paper,
kick pleat swirl of a skirt.
White ashes clouded the radio, snow and more
snow, ghost
step of a tune
traced the linoleum, faint as wallpaper,
faint
as a dressmaker's mark.
Neat was the house, the rooms
tended well by the broom, the mop, the hands
that plowed flour
under acres of bread,
tidy loaves trim as the beds upstairs.
White ashes feathered weightless as the dream
before the first
snowfall, a glimmering
lifting the body out of the one that sleeps.
White ashes hovered, bountiful air
surrounding.
The temperature, silver
and falling, gauged the icicle's
tear
hauling the moon and the stars.
Snow

and more snow turning the bread, the tins, the basket,
the turning of beds, the turning
always away
and toward the door.
Outside a brother hollered, "I'm home!"
White ashes flew off the boots that drifted past
dusk, blizzards
across the chalkboard
heaped the work of hours
onto spoons.
Too soon!
Outside a brother hollered,
knocking snow
off his boots, knocking his name at the door.
"I'm home!"
A geography of ice
lit the screen,
a map pulled down like a windowshade.
The classroom collapsed into black.
Outside snow and more snow and the white
glare before the countdown,
the numbers
spooling through the heat of projection,
frame by frame,
out of focus
as the ill-fated expedition in an old newsreel.
A dismal documentary,
reports due back on Monday.
White ashes freckled the coats, the collars, the sleeves
of children falling
into hedges of snow.
Wingless insects, lichen and moss lost
in theory,
the continental drift and the myth of frozen
oceans.

The explorers, however, remained forever fur laden, forever
turning and waving,
turning toward the snow.
Outside a brother hollered,
"Snow!"
Neat was the house, the rooms, and the beds,
the mathematics of pie tins
fluctuating
once temperatures soared, golden
and rising, cherries
jellying into dimestore lipstick, the body
rising to stun
a glacier,
bring the explorers home.
The pie tins, mirrored like Mexican
silver, bracelets
linked and charmed, all the trinkets hammered
to outlast us—the pie tins, talced and primed
for sweetness—
a young girl's face
sudden in the first incoherent
white kiss of blossoms burning the orchard with lace,
moth clouds
and
laundry,
fields of white shirts,
standard and starched,
issued at birth,
an army of brothers marched through.

The Land of Bliss

Why give me light
and then this dark without a dawn?
  —*Joni Mitchell*

The Last of My Chinese Uncles Enters the Gates of Heaven

and my mother, unable to weep, sits outside a room of memory
where all her tears are stored.

I watch my mother among the mourners
who have come to bury the dead.
Today the dead happens to be my uncle.
My uncle was one of many orphans who climbed back into this life,
and did not drown.

My mother enters an old grief that binds
her to the compassionate soup
of those who took her in.
She slips through the old woman
she has become out of the mother she lost and into the child
who waited quietly on the other side of the door.

She heard the widows' earthly cries,
sounds she clung to as she fell
past windows cluttered with buckets and knives.
Hands, shouting into the water, shouting into my mother,
tore through laundry linking tenements.

The widows made their way to the river on broken feet.
They made a rope of hands and pulled a small child
into this life.
My mother gulped grief and drowned.

The widows urged her to gnaw the scrawny
wings of chicken to put meat on her bones.
Eat, *the widows cried.*
Eat and live.
Such exhortations bound her to the earthly gristle.

Hands by way of the river bound the body of my grandmother
in plain white cloth.
Hands by way of the river carried my mother into this life.

The widows' tinctures—the roots, the berries, the twigs, and
the leaves—failed to calm my grandmother's body.
If my mother could trace the festering
she could say the wound started here
in the smallest rung of the spine.
When my grandmother climbed the ladder
to enter heaven, a petal
fluttered toward the child who waited for her mother to appear
one last time and make known
in one form or another
her death and her life.
The door clanged shut like the lid on a pot.
The widows lit incense, sickly coils of sweetness
to mask the scent,
and wailed.

I enter the story by way of the river,
enter the sequence in a reversal of falling.
One ghost life to another.

Hands by way of the story reach to tell it for her.

The widows hobbled on broken feet—
what the living and the dead require—
to wrap the dead in plain white cloth,
the living in the earthly broth.
They reached into death, the pull
and tug, and lifted a strand from the river.
Broken feet,
knotted hands
braided a rope towards the body's life.

My mother sits quietly on the other side of the door.
I wait for my mother to appear
and make herself known to me.

Hands by way of the story reach for her.

The dying leave a scent.
A child follows it
heavenward.
Incense drapes the room.
No earthly broom can sweep
enough ashes into our hands.

The day one is saved from falling
another child drowns.

Human life is a wound that will not heal.

She grabbed the rope and entered
this life,
a river of rags and sorrow.

She closes her eyes and binds herself to the scent
that flutters through her body like a passage
of silk entering the gates of heaven.

Hands by way of the story want to bring us home.

Weep, my hands shout.
Weep and live.

Triptych

The young master, in order to share his joy,
comes down from the mountain.
He rents a modest room
and sets up shop
amid the tenements of passionate life—
bickering neighbors, scalded children,
the love cries of reckless couplings,
the eternal sadness of halfhearted suppers.
With an immigrant's singleness of purpose,
he waits.
He vows to wait for as long as it takes.
He waters the flowers, dusts the sign, bows
ten thousand times.
In the flickering gloom of the neon
bar across the way,
he watches the hungry ghosts
piggyback humankind,
endlessly riding free—
the smoking ghost, the gambling ghost,
the drinking ghost, the laughing ghost,
the crying ghost, the demon ghost, the jealous ghost,
the ghost of fear, the victim ghost, the abuser
ghost, the ghost of countless possessions,
the ghost of chilling arrogance, the killing
ghost, the manic ghost, the panic ghost, the master
ghost of deception,
the ghost of shame,
the ghost of pornography,
the constipated ghost, the vomit ghost,
the ghost of nail biting, scab picking, ass scratching,
dandruff eating, snot sucking, pimple squeezing,
chocolate hoarding, glue sniffing,
child beating, woman hating, self-loathing
ghost upon ghost upon ghost—

ghosts of past karmic evil so profound
endlessly riding free,
and no one seems to mind.

The young master resolves to dig deeper
in order to share his joy
with each hunger
that manifests through the door.
He waits,
and radiates true and real sincerity.
Given the right conditions,
a ghost can be distracted, pacified
as if sexually satisfied,
and a humankind, say, a woman, an ordinary
housewife, inextricably
attracted to the light,
finds the courage to sneak away,
climb the stairs, break past
the ghost who would tie her to the bed,
tie her to the stove,
hurl her typewriter out the window,
smash her sculptures against the wall.
All indecencies gloat, belly up,
raggedy, maggoty, obscenely cheerful.
The ghost sleeps, dead
to the world, an opening she seizes,
a thread of spittle across the pillow.
Into the dream of the young master
she makes a run for it.
Long before her footsteps have entered his mind,
her existence has already been known.
He fixes his mind upon the rotten honeycomb,
intricate rooms carved like a temple,
flies at the altar,
sweetness abandoned.

He prepares a sun-warmed stone
to heat a cold and fearful abdomen.
Love begins here,
a stone made tender
at the moment of acceptance.
He tiptoes around her,
lets her
come closer.
He knows the fragility of human aspiration—
the housewife has been feeling so
bad for so long,
he is careful not to frighten her.
The slightest gesture of kindness
causes her to burst into tears.
The slightest pressure to change
causes her to flee.
The young master sits and waits.

Frantic at first,
the ghost wakes up to find her missing
and screams bloody murder.
Where the hell were you?
Every day she returns.
Tactic number two,
the ghost cries and coos,
I love you, I love you, I love you.
Every day she returns,
everyday she gets warmer.
Tactic number three,
the ghost whispers,
Baby, you ain't nothin' without me.
The young master waters the flower.
Number four,
I'll kick you out the door.
Every day she returns.
Number five,
I'll bury you alive.

Everyday she grows stronger.
Number six,
I'll break your bones into sticks.
Loving kindness awaits within her.
Number seven,
I'll stuff you in the oven.
Number eight,
I'll crush you with my weight.
Number nine,
Baby, I'm yours, you're mine,
the chill crawling along the spine.
Tactic number ten,
I'll worm my way into you again.
Every day she returns,
everyday they grow closer.
In exile she blooms
forgiveness,
that dreaded odor
arising out of the mud of curses and complaints.
At last the ghost lets go,
looking to hitch an easier fuck.
Fortunate to be born into human life,
she breathes the peace that awaits within her—
cherishes the infant asleep on a lotus petal.
The young master bows ten thousand times.

The Bodhisattva Muses

The compassionate one is grateful to us for another life.
She practices her art, and we return
her roses with poems arising out of nights of clarity.
The tranquil ascension of mind equals the depths to which
she has suffered.
She can rest now unhindered by memory.
She has earned this, we say, mindful of our negligence
when we failed to guard her beauty as she was developing her light.
We miscalculated the effort it would take
for the compassionate one to transform the two into full power.

The compassionate one calls it an act of kindness.
If only she knew we were saving ourselves, resuscitating
those whom we had once long ago chosen for the art,
those capable of obsession or devotion.
The child who draws a thousand pictures in the dirt,
markings that resemble birds or sharks, demons or storms,
is the same child who washes her hands each time she opens a door.
Our visitations had been infrequent, our infusions feeble.
We gave strength to her voice in a house without shelter.
There was no place safe in which to sing.
How could she offer us roses, we cry, when she could barely feed herself?

The compassionate one claims she heard our first appeal
one Sunday morning. We were the ladies in the choir
calling to her, singing about the Lamb of God.
Knowing what she knew by then led her down the aisle.
She was the lamb whose chance had come to declare herself
someone else's daughter.
The congregation bore witness to her betrayal of the father.

The singing turned rapturous by the time the compassionate one
had placed herself into the fold.
Praise the Lord, the mother cried, nibbling redemption
without effort, like a candy bar, without
betraying complicity in the father's nightly trespasses.
Praise the Lord, the mother cried, and the crumbs fell out of her mouth.

We appear mysteriously in many forms.
Perhaps we were those singing ladies who appealed
to the compassionate one's need for devotion.
She sought shelter and we answered, in retrospect, feebly
—the form of a father
she hungered for, a sheltering god who struck hard
with a crush so deep she began writing
love letters in a diary of imitation leather.
On the cover, embossed in gold, shined the year of her conversion.
Her first poems, congested as the onion skin pages of the black Bible
she was given that day, flew out the window, love letters
we should have intercepted
before the arrival of the boy who talked tenderly, more sweetly
than any god or father, who talked her into giving
what we didn't know had already been taken.

Surely she would have burned the pages of her diary
in a fiery display had the boy not given her heaven
in a patch of grass beyond the cemetery, a nest
he cleared of cigarette stems and bottle shards,
what she was running toward when her father's curses
reached her, pelted her ribs, and knocked her down.

Slow to awaken to danger, we still did not intervene.
Even when the boy treated her badly,
we allowed, for the sake of art, the boy to break her heart.
Through suffering she would become her own subject.
Through words she would heal her way back,

become stronger, more interesting—remade, pieced by hand,
and humanly flawed.

Through that open window came those who said
they loved her knew what was best for her and in laying
those tender claims insisted she relinquish her light.
A poet, one whose failings had yet to turn sour, saw his chance
at beauty.
Pinned under the blade of his windshield,
a love letter had fluttered out of that open window.
The girl had promise. He flailed at the light.
The poet, a tinkerer of the third tier, inserted himself between the lines.
The girl had promise.
So began the poet's pursuit of the voice
he thought he heard singing in a tree outside his window.
He wanted to bring the voice
into his room, stash it under his pillow,
reduce it to a whisper.
Only then would she sing for him.
The girl had promise.

Light was catching up to beauty.
We had to work quickly.
We vowed to surround the compassionate one
with passionate attention.
We inflicted addiction—writing as an act of existence.
Only when words struck the page did an experience
become manifest.
The interference of her words to brutal experience
a shield others took as insolence, standoffishness.
When she was called selfish by those who said
they loved her knew what was best for her, we breathed
a chorus of exhortation
to defy without heartlessness.
We did not want a heart of stone.
We wanted poems.

We failed to give her our protection
during the time of the gathering of the light.
Those who said they loved her knew
what was best for her grew jealous of her solitude.
We failed to give her our protection
when we did not shelter her in her father's house,
a father who could fuck his own daughter and proudly
show the caseworker his handiwork, his baby—
two hits in one, both daughter and granddaughter—
how do you like that?—
heaven in this godforsaken hellhole,
something to keep him happy in his old age.
There is no place to sing
except somewhere down the road out in the woods,
but by then she is skittish, afraid of any enclosure.

Through that open window came those who said
they loved her knew what was best for her and in laying
those tender claims insisted she be like the rest of them.
These clever ones are no less dangerous
than those who screech to a halt to extinguish
any sign of beauty growing on the side of the road.
They can't stand the sight of it.
The sign of the touched.
Such beauty only makes them feel more gruesome in such light.
So wrong were we to think she could sing
in that house when outside there are men
loitering in the garage
and the party takes a twisted turn into insults,
broken glass, something breaking.
A form of fishing and hunting
done with all those spare parts
scattered around the yard—
what else do you do with heartlessness?—
all those spare parts and all that spare time.

Mother of Us All

Mother of the long silences
that pinned us to our chairs,
where were you in your body
if not here with us?

Mother of the stolen roses
that faded like kisses,
why so pale by the window,
peering in at us?

Mother of the prayer beads
that pooled on our pillows,
what were you murmuring,
hands like paper pressed from us?

Mother of the snakes
that coiled around each wrist,
did it ever occur to you to poison us?

Mother of the mirrors
that disassembled the walls,
how many times did we see you look beyond us?

Mother of the incessant purges
that sent our beautiful books and toys to charity,
what perfect world had you not already given us?

Mother of the busy hands
that tore at the spiked tongues,
what were you pulling, hiding at dusk from us?

Mother of the white hair
that sprouted overnight,
what made you skittish,
lock every door behind us?

Mother of the diminishing voice
that broke into chalk,
how could we have known there were things
you had wanted to tell us?

Mother of the disappearance
that shadowed Father's face,
when did you decide you had to leave us.

Out of the Broken Mirror

At the slender
feet of the compassionate
one, ants
string offerings, thread
a garland of rotten
fruit, flesh
of the useful ones, humble
jewels,
these backyard fruit.

Out of the broken
mirror, papaya spills
ovarian seeds, tender
flesh after a hysterectomy.

Empty, the body
shapes itself
into a pouch of skin.

Now you are nothing.
Now you exist.

The compassionate
one accepts the piss of liquor,
smoke, tinfoiled
bits of sweets, accepts
what is placed at her feet.

A wish for happiness
in the life to come.

No one brings her
vegetables. A tomato,
sincerely placed,
is entirely honorable.

Your mother grew
graveyard flowers.
Humble jewels,
these backyard flowers.

Into your room
we bring
your mother's flowers.

A wish for happiness
in the life to come.

Out of the broken
mirror, sand
shatters the hourglass
and a waterfall of time
pours all the years
you spent in the desert.

The tumor ripens,
sucks the sunlight
from your cheeks.

Why were you
gone so long?
We gave you
up for dead.
We are glad
to see you.

Empty, your room
waits, cool
with the scent of lemons
lifting the memory
of your mother's apron.

Out of the broken
mirror, your father
has gone to fetch you.
No lover to see
you through this life.
No child to see
you through the next.
Your father has gone
to fetch you.

A wish for happiness
in the life to come.

Even though you have
nothing
to say,
we are glad
you are back.
Everything
is as it was
when you left.
Your room is
just as
it has always been,
tended well as an altar,
scrubbed clean as an infirmary.

Into your room
we bring your mother's flowers.

Lie down.
Rest.
You look so tired.

Now you are nothing.
Now you exist, adorned
with the fragrance of light.

All the flowers of childhood
were flowers for the grave.

Tender flesh,
empty the broken
body empty
the broken heart.

Your father has gone
to fetch you.
Gone into his broken
heart. A hole
in the sand and all the years
to fill it.
A wish for happiness
in the life to come.

Angels on the Way to the Dalai Lama

You open a window of ferns
today after a long illness
and in the soft green shadows

of moss-light unfurling the curled
furred tongues you feel
the feathered voices of the women

who have brought you here.
Women who step in beside you and walk
a way with you on your way

to something bigger, not knowing
in that simple moment
beside a canefield and a dusty road

that what she offers
is seamless as breathing,
each step of her story, carried like a hundred

years on her back, reclaiming
the orphan she once was, ironing
a mountain of handkerchiefs

for the monsignor in the mansion.
She is hungry, and so are you,
as you reach into your pocket

for the apple she accepts
because each step is a red
thread to the possibilities

of every beginning, spiraling
now in the lotus peel
of the fruit unspooling in your hands.

She is for you another angel
taking place beside you
on a red dirt road, a light in the wind,

a light rustling, shaking
the dust off the eyelids
of your feet.

How small your steps until now.
And in the generosity of their stories,
you lift your face full to the sky.

Clouds sail past,
a clustering of notes, engaging
and dismantling, the bright square

knots you have been stuck holding.

Handful

Like scooping water by the handful
out of a lake,
you write a poem,
contain it, gaze
into the small
cup of your hand.
While you admire
what feels cold and impossibly
clear, unlike anything
you've ever held before,
you still did not get it.
Into the momentary displacement
left by the dipping of your hand
flows more.

Caldera Illumina

She came to regard the house of rain falling as her muse.
She removed her shoes before entering the house.
She did not want to bring into the house hungry ghosts.
She had seen what happens when the muse is left to die,
roofs collapsing into kitchens, women at windows staring
out of caves.
They hang no curtains, their faces already hidden.
They do not have the strength to muster up
the evil eye.
Still, she runs from them, hiding the roses under her coat,
the roses
she will place in every room of the house,
once she has shut the door behind her.

She wanted nothing in the house to interfere with her work.
She began to work again.

She began to thrash, hauling a body of language into the house,
an assemblage of parts—parts of speech, parts of dreams.
Across the structure of bone she stretched gut,
pulled transparent.
She crouched, spooling what came pouring out,
crude structures that remained
mute as oracles.
She had to go as far as possible.
She had to take the body of language
to near death.

So much of her wanted air.
The claims upon her kept her bound to those who could not live
without her.
Across the structure of bone she stretched gut,
poked holes
for the crude thing to breathe.
She knew the language of smoke,
wrapped breath to link the confluence of wind, rock,

and mist.
Along the crater rim in that hour between night and day,
speech and dreams,
joy and grief,
she walked into a light rain falling.

She had seen the bats gather at dusk beneath the hills.
Clouds of them convening, dragging
an awkward scrawl
across the sky.

In expectation she left herself open.
She walked into places she should have left
unspoken
without dragging the broken language through groves
built for
worship.

The stone that caught her eye,
the one that called out to her from all the others,
was the one that bewitched,
was the one she brought home.

Across the body of language something clawed
at her breath
so that her breath,
lured like a bat out of the trees,
pursuing the stone's disruption in its blind field,
disintegrated.
A gush of wings broke gravity,
collided with mistaken fruit.
She could not make a sound.
Into her presence it clawed its inarticulate matter.
Into her sleep it flew repeatedly,
like rain battering a windshield.
She howled herself back into night,
moonless and eternal.

Prospering beyond the waking apparent she walked,
talking to the self she came to believe was reliable,
like the one who called her every day
who leaked lies back to her, crowding out with compliments
the other true ally
who asks nothing of you,
for what you have to tell
says nothing that is not already known.

Calling herself back with the strength of her voice
awakens her.
She begins to fortify herself against that which descends at night
to steal it.
She begins to hide the voice in the rooms of the house,
taking it out of its fur-lined case.

She knows if she can find her—find the girl
who had the presence of mind to dig a hole
when it became apparent
she was lost from the others
near nightfall on the high slopes of the volcano,
a hole that sheltered her from the wind, the plummeting temperatures,
and buried herself in it—she can find what is required
to remain alive,
the will
to descend and dig a hole in the earth
with bare hands.

Across the structure of bone she stretches gut,
bandages,
and ropes of skin
spooling at her feet.
She begins to sing,
humming far back in her throat,
a frequency inaudible at the time of construction,
given body
at the recitation of another mouth

surrounding moss, fur, feathers until
it is one mouth speaking one word at a time.

At any moment she can enter the story and find herself
having already entered the room, the house falling with rain.
The clairvoyance of rooms
opens its scent, pressing light upon the temple
so that a dream's fragment
remains throughout the day and all her days,
blue with the roses of the sea she leapt from as a child
safe on the high cliff of her father's shoulders,
the blue roses of clouds
pouring rain into her sleep.

The first time she slept in the house the numbers of the clock
dripped like a swollen candle the night blew out.
The hours pooled at her feet.
Out of her throat
came pure lozenges that slipped into the night waters
like tears
the shape of fish.

The secret of the roses
was in the ashes she carried in her hands
to mark the places where blue, vibrant and clear,
was to appear.

Nowhere to go but deeper into the darkest room.
All else is failure, a pile of last year's mail to sort.
She could spend all the days of her waking sifting through
shiny paper and feel she is peeling away toward
the core of something permanent.
She is distraction itself, and into her light
she draws obstacles to keep herself from entering
the last room.

She was the house, the house on fire, flames
leaping from windows inexplicable as the words that illumined

her mind.
She burnished miniature gold leaves
in a fountain of ink.
So the evening's book of hours
unfurled
leaf by leaf,
the ladder's green stem
she climbed to enter the house, the room, the bed
she lay in as a child
watching the torn wallpaper swirl like gray snow from the ceiling.

She left the fire burning in the house.
She left the house glowing in the forest.
She left the forest not knowing
she would return to sift through roses.

What she carried out of the house
was the poultice of smoke and ruin
festering until the moment she entered the last room
fluid, unencumbered.

In the recovery process the patient will begin to doubt
her version of the story.
This is to be expected.
In fact, necessary, given the structure of material.

Somewhere there is the mother whose help you will seek.
And she will not be able to help you.
She cannot help herself.
And the truth of it is painful.

The house, luminous, generous, opened for her an unsettling.
What flew into the window flew out the skylight.
It too was passing through.

Somewhere there is the father whose distance you must keep.
And he will try to exert his will.
He cannot help himself.

And the truth of it is final.
So passing she enters rooms to ignite the familiar
like the stove she lights in the morning.
One day the flame jumps to attention,
simply itself,
a coil of heat to bring water to air—
an act of transformation that will, in fact, occur
without her.

Across the structure of bone she stretches gut,
her senses
hit by years of rot.
In this way she begins to compose the minutiae,
the extraneous, the cluttering, still fluttering, she was, however,
moving inward.

In writing this she knows she is courting danger,
opening herself up
to the black stretch of road.
At every turn distraction
exists to steal her happiness.
She begins to work some kind of wreckage of bone and gut.
She swerves to meet the apparition,
and her eventual arrival.

Two hours left before her return to the world.
The rain keeps falling, the roses weep.
The house has an expectant loneliness of table and chairs.
The wind dwells in the stove, cold with her burning
when she went into the last room.
Two hours left before her return, and still she is gone.
The clock ticks worry.
Two hours left and she has yet
to appear.
The rain gathers years into its falling.
Drink,
rain of childhood,
once you were a cloud.

Out of her window words fly—
candle, cave, church, chair,
breath, bruise, moss, air,
the mind wills the hands—
insect, infinite—
the typist sings one note at a time.
Beyond the light of the kitchen window she steps outside.
She crouches in smoke.
She flicks a match beyond the boundary of the familiar—
insignificant, magnificent—
a juncture between two parts,
speech and dream, bone and gut, two edges of a single crisis—
incision, inscription—and looks up.
The music she hears is what she brings to the night.
The stars appear on schedule.

She approaches sleep like a drug,
night softening the length of her spine,
or a country where attendants greet her, gather her
into a fur of darkness,
feathering her eyelids with the blessings of the blind.
Night takes her hand and walks her down
its corridors, past rooms of gardens of scentless
flowers—no tissue of memory quickens there—
to a room where only sound can reach her.
The human voice requires nothing of space.
The purest note,
fused to a drop of sound—
hovering as if at the edge of sound—
becomes a lake,
cold and blue and vast.

Across the structure she burns the last stick of wood.
Not a shred of combustible material remains.
She has finished her work.
She has burned without regret
what is already done.

The child awakens having suffered a blow to the head
and opens her eyes to a country
where dark plumes of smoke
rise like statues in the fallen air.
Out of the years and the rain she walks toward you,
walks toward you with a certainty
you are somehow known to each other.
You have been there, haven't you—which was your room?
Did we walk past each other, past the garden of scentless
flowers, past the quiet cleanliness of nuns?
Did we swim in the night waters of the lake?
The child gathers the petals
into her small bed—
a place from which no one
had thought to retrieve her—
and in the hour before the sun
feathers the hills, light praising the trees,
longing is matched by beauty
in the singing that carries her to the hospital
balcony
where she opens, let's say, her heart,
to a sound she knew existed
somewhere in this world.

The Land of Bliss

Rain that falls and has been falling
is the same rain that fell
a million years ago. To think not
a single droplet has been lost
in the articulate
system of our blue planet
wrapped in its gauze of atmosphere.
Like breathing, the planetary breath
draws oceans, rivers, lakes,
and even these ponds,
cradling gold fish.

After a night of rain, the benevolent eye
of morning glistens a fine mesh
between ferns.

Last night I climbed the ladder
to the loft, tired in a way the bones
liquify after a day of doing
the work one has set out to do.
I had worked mindful and steady through the hours
on a poem not quite done.

The thought that there would be
more work of the same to do
when I woke up,
that there would be
that poem waiting,
made me happy.

I sank into bed, cradled by the sound
of rain filling the night: wet leaves
and old gold ponds.

I drifted before entering the body of sleep,
the breathing slowing down to a quiet
web of vibration, quiet
to the point of stillness,
as if I held my breath to swim
toward dreams waiting on the other shore.

The Pure Land is empty.
There's nobody there.

Acknowledgments

"Pokanini Girl" is for Eric Chock and Darrell Lum.

"Stink Eye" is for Tamara Wong Morrison and Rachel Davenport.

"The Child Floats in a Sea of Grass" is for Joy Kobayashi and Xander Cintron.

"What Is Given" is for Joshua Davenport.

"Fetters" is for Reverend and Mrs. Toshio Murakami.

"She Meant to See China" and "The Valley Boat" are for Wing Tek Lum.

"In the Far Wing of an Old Museum" is for Jeffrey Hantover and Mee Seen Loong.

"A City of Sleeves" is for Wayne Morioka and Andrea Song Gelber.

"Triptych" is for Jung Hoon Lee.

"Angels on the Way to the Dalai Lama" is for Juliet S. Kono and Lee Kyselka.

"Handful" is for Ron Offen.

"Caldera Illumina" is for Sara Nunes.

"The Land of Bliss" is for Sets Takashige, Arthur Kaufman and Kinji Kanazawa.

Grateful acknowledgment is made to the editors of the following publications, where the following poems first appeared (some in slightly different versions):

Blueline ("The Child Floats in a Sea of Grass"); *The Carolina Quarterly,* fall/winter 1998 ("The Last of My Chinese Uncles Enters the Gates of Heaven"); *Crab Orchard Review* ("Honored Guest," "Horizon," "In the Far Wing of an Old Museum," "My Mother's Name," "The Roses of Guadalajara," "What is Given"); *Five Points,* vol. 3, no. 2 ("A Poet in the House"); *Free Lunch* ("Committed," "Handful," "Stone Soup"); *Hybolics* ("Out of the Broken Mirror"); *Kenyon Review* ("The Girl Can Run," "The Sky-Blue Dress," "The Slow Upheaval of Mist," "Stink Eye"); *Meridian* ("Fragrance Is the First to Go"); *Michigan Quarterly Review* ("Book of Hours," spring 2000, "Fetters," spring 1999, "The Pineapple Fields," fall 1996); *New England Review* ("Blue"); *Poetry*

Ireland Review ("Angels on the Way to the Dalai Lama,"); *Southern Review* ("Pa-ke," "Riverbed," "The Valley Boat").

"Ghost" originally appeared in the 1994 Fall/Winter volume of the *Asian Pacific American Journal* by the Asian American Writers' Workshop.

"The Land of Bliss" and "She Meant to See China" were previously published in *Bamboo Ridge, Journal of Hawai'i Literature and Arts,* issue number 75. "A City of Sleeves" and "Triptych" were previously published in *Bamboo Ridge,* issue number 77. "Living Proof" and "Pokanini Girl" were previously published in *Bamboo Ridge,* issue number 79.

"The Expense of Mildew" and "Peacefully, on the Wings of Forgiveness," first appeared in *Meridians:* feminism, race, transnationalism, vol. 1, no. 1 (November 2000).

"Mountains of Ash" originally appeared in *New Letters,* volume 65, number 2 (winter 1999). It is reprinted here with permission of *New Letters* and the Curators of the University of Missouri-Kansas City.

"Blueroses," "Fur," "Mother of Us All," "Rust," and "White Ashes" are reprinted from *Shenandoah:* The Washington and Lee University Review, with the permission of the Editor.

"The Bodhisattva Muses," "Caldera Illumina," and "The Sister" were previously published in *The Quietest Singing* (Hawai'i State Foundation on Culture and the Arts, 2000).

"Mother of Us All" appears in *The Best American Poetry 2000.*
"The Sky-Blue Dress" was awarded *The Pushcart Prize XXIV,* 2000.

I am indebted to Taitetsu Unno and his book, *River of Fire, River of Water.*
I wish to thank the National Endowment for the Arts for support during the writing of this book.

The Land of Bliss is Cathy Song's fourth book of poetry. Her first, *Picture Bride*, was the winner of the 1982 Yale Series of Younger Poets Award and was nominated for a National Book Critics Circle Award. Her other books are *Frameless Windows, Squares of Light* and *School Figures*. Song's poetry has been widely anthologized in such publications as *Boomer Girls: Poems by Women from the Baby Boom Generation, The Morrow Anthology of Younger American Poets, The Norton Anthology of American Literature,* and *The Norton Anthology of Modern Poetry*. Her poems have also appeared on the buses of Atlanta, the subway cars of New York, the *Poetry Daily* website, and, most recently, in *The Best American Poetry 2000*. She is the recipient of numerous awards, including the Frederick Bock Prize from *Poetry,* the Shelly Memorial Award from the Poetry Society of America, the Hawaii Award for Literature, a fellowship from the National Endowment for the Arts, and a Pushcart Prize. Song earned a B.A. from Wellesley College and an M.A. from Boston University. She was born in Honolulu, Hawaii, where she lives with her husband and three children.

The Land of Bliss was designed and typeset in Dante MT
with Cataneo BT display type by Kachergis Book Design,
Pittsboro, North Carolina.